Cambridge English Readers
....
Level 2

Includes 2 CDs - CD
Series editor: Philip Prowse
Missir
2

The New Zealand File

Richard MacAndrew

CAMBRIDGE
UNIVERSITY PRESS

CAMBRIDGE UNIVERSITY PRESS
Cambridge, New York, Melbourne, Madrid, Cape Town, Singapore, São Paulo, Delhi

Cambridge University Press
The Edinburgh Building, Cambridge CB2 8RU, UK

www.cambridge.org
Information on this title: www.cambridge.org/9780521136242

First published 2009

Richard MacAndrew has asserted his right to be identified as the Author of the Work in
accordance with the Copyright, Designs and Patents Act 1988.

Printed in India by Replika Press Pvt. Ltd

Illustrations by Paul Dickinson
Map artwork by Malcolm Barnes

A catalogue record of this book is available from the British Library.

ISBN 978-0-521-13624-2 paperback
ISBN 978-0-521-13628-0 paperback plus audio CD

No character in this work is based on any person living or dead.
Any resemblance to an actual person or situation is purely accidental.

With thank   *d, as always,*
thanks to P   *nd advice.*

Contents

Chapter 1	From Fiji to Christchurch	6
Chapter 2	Christchurch	11
Chapter 3	From Christchurch to Haast	15
Chapter 4	Queenstown	19
Chapter 5	Wanaka – morning	24
Chapter 6	Wanaka – afternoon	28
Chapter 7	From Wanaka to Dunedin	34
Chapter 8	Dunedin	39
Chapter 9	The end of the road	43

People in the story

Ian Munro:
a British spy working
for British Intelligence

Naylor:
Ian Munro's boss

Cochrane:
another British spy
working for British
Intelligence

Lisa Jardine:
a nurse in Wanaka,
New Zealand

Places in the story

Chapter 1   *From Fiji to Christchurch*

Ian Munro was lying on a beach on the Fijian island of Viti Levu. The sun was hot and the sea was warm and blue. Next to him a tall beautiful Fijian woman was putting sun oil on her long dark legs.

'This is the life,' Munro thought to himself.

Just then a man with a phone in his hand ran along the beach from Munro's hotel. He was wearing a white shirt and dark trousers – one of the hotel workers.

'Mr Munro! Mr Munro!' he called.

Munro sat up.

'Telephone, Mr Munro,' said the man, giving Munro the phone. 'Your father. He says it's important.'

'Thank you,' said Munro. He took the phone. 'Hello?'

'Munro,' said a voice that Munro knew well. It was Naylor, his boss.

'Hello, Dad,' said Munro.

'Forget the jokes,' said Naylor. 'Are you with someone?'

'Yes,' replied Munro.

'I know you're on holiday. But I need you. Are you free?'

'No, but I can be,' replied Munro.

'Good,' said Naylor. 'Get yourself to New Zealand. There's a plane tonight to Christchurch. Your ticket will be at the airport. Cochrane will meet you at Christchurch airport. You know Cochrane?'

Munro did know Cochrane. He always had a lot to say for himself. Too much, actually, thought Munro.

'Yes,' he answered.

'Good,' said Naylor again. 'He'll find you at the airport. And he'll tell you what the job is.'

Munro smiled to himself. Naylor never left Britain on business or on holiday.

'Any questions?' asked Naylor.

'No,' said Munro. Naylor finished the call. Munro looked at the woman next to him. Then he spoke into the phone again.

'Oh no! That's terrible,' he said. 'Yes, of course I can. I'll get a plane as soon as I can … OK, Dad … Yes … Yes … I'll call you from the airport … OK. Bye.'

He turned off the phone and kissed the woman softly.

'Sorry, my dear,' he said. 'I've got to go. My grandmother's very ill.'

'Oh Ian!' she said, looking up at him with a half-smile on her face. 'Every time you come to Fiji one of your family gets ill and you have to leave early. What is wrong with all you Munros?'

Munro laughed.

'I'll call you,' he said, touching the side of her face. Then he stood up and started walking along the beach.

* * *

Twelve hours later Munro's plane arrived at Christchurch airport. Munro watched out of the window as the plane moved across to the airport buildings. Fiji was a wonderful place, but it was good to get back to work.

Munro was one of a number of people who worked for British Intelligence. Many years ago people called them spies. Today they were 'foreign executives'. Same job, different name.

Cochrane was waiting for him, a small bag in his hand, a smile on his face. He was wearing a dark brown jacket and light brown trousers. He looked like someone who sold used cars.

'Good holiday?' he asked. 'Fiji, I hear. Lovely place, lovely people.'

'Yes,' said Munro.

'Let's get a coffee, shall we?' said Cochrane. 'Then I'll tell you what the old man's got for you.'

Naylor? The old man? Munro smiled to himself. He couldn't see Naylor liking that.

Five minutes later they were sitting at a table in a corner of the airport coffee shop. Munro looked around at the other people. Cochrane saw him.

'Hey! Come on, Munro,' he said, laughing a little. 'I can do my job, you know. Nobody followed me here.'

Munro said nothing. He just waited for Cochrane to begin.

Cochrane put his bag on the table and opened it. He started taking things out and putting them in front of Munro.

'Map of New Zealand,' he said. 'Car keys. I'll show you the car when we've finished here. Phone. My number is in the address book. Address of safe house.' He gave Munro a piece of paper. 'Nobody knows about this place except you and me. And the old man, of course. Remember the address and give me back the paper.' Munro read the address twice and then passed it back to Cochrane.

Cochrane showed Munro a photo of a man – just the head and shoulders. The man had short fair hair and blue eyes. He was wearing a light blue shirt, open at the neck.

'Longstaffe,' said Cochrane. 'One of ours. Do you know him?'

'I know who he is,' said Munro. 'I don't think I've ever spoken to him.'

'That's OK,' said Cochrane putting away the photo. 'He knows who you are too. He's a good man.'

Cochrane shut his bag and drank some of his coffee.

'Well,' he said. 'This is the job. Go to Haast Beach …' He started to open the map, but Munro stopped him.

'It's OK,' said Munro. 'I've been here before. I know where Haast Beach is.'

'Oh!' Cochrane stopped speaking for a moment. Then he went on: 'Well, Haast Beach. Longstaffe's coming in there

9

at one o'clock tomorrow night from a Norwegian ship. The ship is on its way back home from Antarctica. You meet Longstaffe and take him to the safe house in Queenstown. Longstaffe has some important information and we need to make sure he, and the information, is safe.'

'And then?' asked Munro.

'Then … I don't know.' Cochrane smiled. 'You wait and see. I only found out about this job yesterday morning. I've done everything Naylor asked me to so far: car, phone, safe house, meeting you. I don't know what happens next – but when I do, I'll let you know.'

'OK,' said Munro. 'And why the meeting on the beach? Why doesn't Longstaffe just take a plane to Christchurch like everyone else who's in a hurry to leave Antarctica?'

'Something to do with the information he has,' said Cochrane. 'A lot of other people want it, I believe. Better for Longstaffe if not too many people know where he is. You know what I mean?'

Munro didn't reply. He finished his coffee. First he turned the phone off and put it in his pocket. He didn't like mobile phones. Sometimes you really needed them. The problem was that when you turned them on, people could find out where you were. Next he put the map in the side pocket of his bag. Then he took the car keys off the table.

'OK. Where's the car?' he asked.

* * *

Ten minutes later Munro was driving along the main road from the airport to the city. Two minutes after that he knew he had a problem. A large dark blue car was following him – and there were two people inside.

Chapter 2 *Christchurch*

Munro turned left and the blue car followed him. Munro turned right. The car followed again. It wasn't a mistake. The car was following him.

Munro turned back onto the main road into the city. He thought as he drove. He needed to get away. But he also wanted answers to some questions. Who was in the car? Who were they working for? And how had they found him so soon?

Munro drove into Christchurch. In the centre of the city is the beautiful building of ChristChurch Cathedral, built in the late 1800s. As Munro drove past, he saw that there were a lot of tourists around it. Just what he needed – people.

He left his car not far from the cathedral and walked back. Out of the corner of his eye, he saw the blue car stop by the side of the road. A tall dark-haired man got out, wearing jeans, a black T-shirt and a black jacket. He was about fifty metres behind Munro and was talking into his phone. Calling for help, probably. Munro needed to move fast.

Standing by the front door of the cathedral was a group of Japanese tourists. A young Japanese woman was speaking to them. Munro walked quickly past the group and in through the main door. Inside the cathedral he looked around quickly. He didn't have much time. There was a door to the visitors' centre on the left and two young women were just going through it.

On the right was a small room, the Pacific Chapel, with a few seats, and flags and clothes from different Pacific islands: Fiji, Samoa and the Cook Islands. Munro walked across and into the chapel. Now it was difficult for anyone to see him from the main door.

A few moments later the man from the blue car came in through the main door. He stopped and looked around the cathedral, but couldn't see Munro. Then he saw the door to the visitors' centre. Walking across, the man went through the door.

Munro came out of the Pacific Chapel, moved quickly back to the main door and out into the warm December sun. About fifty metres away a man was standing on a chair and speaking. He was wearing a long black coat and a tall black hat. A large group of people was listening to him. Munro remembered this man from his last visit to Christchurch a few years before. He was the Wizard, a strange old man with funny ideas, who often came and spoke to people outside the cathedral. Munro hurried over to this group and then moved in between the people who were listening.

He turned his head and saw his follower come out of the main door of the cathedral. The man looked around everywhere, but didn't see Munro. Munro saw him look at his watch, take out his phone and make a call. Munro turned back to the Wizard. He was talking about his ideas and what he believed. People were asking him questions and laughing at what he said. Munro looked around again and saw his follower start to move away. He was walking down Colombo Street. Munro waited a minute or two and then started walking behind him. Now he was following – and maybe he could get answers to some of his questions.

It is difficult to follow someone at the best of times. When they already know your face, it can be very difficult. For five minutes Munro and the man from the blue car walked along Colombo Street. Munro stayed well back on the other side of the road. The man stopped once to look in a shop window, but soon moved on again. At the corner of Dundas Street, the man stopped again. He looked around. Quickly Munro moved into a shop door. A few moments later he looked out. There was no one there.

Munro ran to the corner and looked along Dundas Street. He was just in time. There was a small street off to the left and the man was turning into it. Munro followed quickly. He turned left after the man. It was a short street with no way out. The man wasn't there. Munro walked along the street looking at the doors. Then he heard a noise behind him. He turned. The man was coming out of a door on Munro's left. He had a knife in his hand.

'You're not so clever after all, are you?' he said. The man spoke English, but it wasn't his first language. Munro couldn't decide where he was from. Eastern Europe, Russia maybe? The man's eyes were cold. He moved easily. 'He likes fighting with a knife,' thought Munro. Munro looked round for help – a piece of wood, anything. Nothing. Slowly the man came closer and closer. Munro watched him carefully, arms out ready. The man moved quickly. His knife hand came out fast, but Munro was faster. He moved outside the man's arm; his right hand took the man's wrist, his left took the man's elbow. He pulled with his right and pushed hard with his left. The knife fell. There was a breaking noise from the man's elbow. He cried out loudly.

Munro pushed the man away. The man turned, his right arm by his side. Munro hit him once hard on the neck with the side of his hand. The man went down. His head hit the ground, his eyes closed. Munro put a hand on the man's neck. He was dead. Quickly Munro looked through the man's pockets. Money, credit cards in the name of Mr A. K. Krikorian, but nothing else – no bills or letters, no passport.

Munro pulled the body to the side of the street so it was difficult to see. Then he walked back and out onto Dundas Street. He turned left onto Colombo Street and walked further away from the cathedral. It was too dangerous now to go back to his car or to the area around the cathedral. A little way along the road there was an office on the left: 'South Island Cars'. Munro went in.

'I need a car,' he said to the woman behind the desk.

Chapter 3 *From Christchurch to Haast*

The drive to Haast was beautiful, but Munro knew it was just one of many beautiful drives in New Zealand. From Christchurch he drove through the mountains over Arthur's Pass to Hokitika. There he stopped and bought some dark clothes to wear that night on the beach. Then he continued down from Hokitika to Haast, with the sea on his right, trees and mountains on his left.

He arrived at Haast at six in the evening and drove down to Haast Beach. There was a small group of buildings, a few cars and a long empty beach. He left his car near the others and went for a walk. All along the beach were pieces of dead tree brought in by the sea. They gave the place a strange feeling. He looked out to sea: three or four fishing boats, but no Norwegian ship. Not yet. He turned to go back to his car and saw two small penguins run into the long grass behind the beach. He went back to his car and drove away. He needed something to eat and to change his clothes.

Later that evening Munro returned to the beach. There was a full moon and it was quite light. Out at sea he could see the lights of a large ship. 'That must be the Norwegian ship with Longstaffe on it,' he thought. Munro found a place in the long grass out of the wind and sat down to wait. He was wearing his dark clothes from Hokitika – black jeans and a black sweater. He looked at his watch from time to time. Then at ten to one he heard the sound of a small boat. He looked up and saw the boat close to the beach.

One man was sitting at the back, another man was getting out.

Munro stood up and looked to the left and the right. The beach was empty. He walked down to the boat.

'Longstaffe?' he asked quietly.

'Yes,' the man replied. 'Good to see you, Munro.'

Longstaffe was wearing dark trousers and a thick dark sweater under a dark jacket. He was carrying a large bag.

Munro took the bag from him.

'Come on,' he said. 'Let's get going.'

Longstaffe waved his thanks to the other man and the boat turned back to the open sea.

Munro and Longstaffe started up the beach. As they got to the long grass, there was the sound of a gun and Longstaffe fell to the ground. Munro went down next to him fast. He put his head up carefully and looked round to see who was shooting. He heard the gun again and something shot through the grass near his head. Quickly he put his head down again.

He looked at Longstaffe. There was blood coming from the side of his mouth. He did not look good.

'Go,' said Longstaffe. 'You go – but take this.' He tried to put his left hand in his pocket, but couldn't.

'Pocket,' he said.

Munro put his hand into the pocket of Longstaffe's jacket and pulled out a small white box. He looked inside. There was a picture card.

'Picture card,' said Longstaffe. He was finding it difficult to speak. 'Important. Penguin. One-eyed penguin.'

'What?' asked Munro. He looked up again, and again someone shot very close to his head. They were somewhere to the left. They knew where he was, but he couldn't see them. His car was over to the right behind a small building, but at the moment he couldn't get there. It was too light.

Munro looked at Longstaffe again.

'What are you talking about?' he asked. But it was too late. Longstaffe was dead.

Munro needed to move. He didn't have a gun, but the men who were shooting at him didn't know that. Not yet anyway. Munro looked at the sky. Hope at last. There were some clouds moving slowly across the sky. Munro put the box in his pocket. He closed Longstaffe's eyes and got ready. A cloud moved across the moon, the beach went dark and

Munro ran. As he ran, he went from side to side a few metres each way. There was more shooting, some close to him. He heard some shouting. 'They've found Longstaffe's body,' he thought. And then he was round the corner, opening his car door and driving away.

Roads in the South Island of New Zealand are usually quiet. At that time of night there are almost no cars on them at all. Munro made good time to Queenstown, arriving soon after five in the morning. The safe house was a flat in a building on Thompson Street. Munro left his car a hundred metres away and walked to the flat. There was no one about and everything was quiet. He passed the front door of the safe house and walked on for another fifty metres. Still quiet. He turned and went back.

There were six flats in the building – two on each floor. The safe house was on the top floor. Munro found the key where Cochrane said it was – in a cleaning cupboard near the front door. He walked up the stairs and let himself in. It was a small flat: one bedroom with two beds, a small kitchen, a bathroom and a living room with a large window. It was just beginning to get light as he looked out of the window. Below him was Lake Wakatipu. He could see the TSS *Earnslaw*, an old ship that took tourists up and down the lake. And on the other side of the lake there was that wonderful line of mountains, the Remarkables.

Just for a moment he remembered what a lovely town this was. But then a large dark car turned into Thompson Street and drove slowly along the road. Munro moved back from the window, but watched the car. It drove past the safe house. Then it turned round, came back a little way and stopped by the side of the road. No one got out.

Chapter 4 *Queenstown*

The living room window looked out of the front of the building, the kitchen window out of the back. Munro went through to the kitchen and looked out over the garden. Behind the garden was another street. And in the street was another dark car. Two large men in dark clothes were getting out and walking up to the door in the back wall of the garden.

'How is this happening?' Munro asked himself. Someone followed him from the airport. Gunmen arrived on Haast Beach when he was meeting Longstaffe. And now the 'safe' house wasn't safe. Who wanted him and how did they know where he was? But this was not really the time for questions. He needed to get away.

Back in the living room he took another look out of the front window. A second car was there now. Two men were getting out of the first car. There was no escape out of the front of the building or the back. There was nowhere to hide inside the flat. Just a cupboard in the bedroom – the first place for anyone to look.

Munro went back to the kitchen. He looked around. And up. What was that? Right above the kitchen table there was a way into the area under the roof.

Munro stood on the table and pushed at the 'door'. It was just a piece of wood about one metre by one. He pushed the wood up and to one side. He was right. It led into the roof.

He got down and looked through the kitchen cupboards. He needed some light up there. He found a torch and turned it on and off. It worked.

Quickly he stood on the table again and pulled himself up into the roof. He put the wood back in place. The roof was not the safest place, but at the moment it was safer than the flat.

Munro turned on the torch and looked around. He was in a large roof area. It was above the safe house flat and also above the other flat on the same floor. Carefully and quietly Munro moved across. Above the other flat he found another door.

'This must go down into next door's kitchen,' he thought. He took up the piece of wood and put it to one side. He looked down. He was right. There were dirty plates and cups on the kitchen table and two empty wine bottles. Someone was living there or staying there. Quietly he let himself down into the kitchen, being careful not to touch anything on the table. He pulled the roof door back into the right place and then got quietly down onto the floor.

He listened. He could hear the sound of people sleeping in the bedroom. But there were also noises from the stairs outside: men coming up, talking in quiet voices.

Munro moved into the living room. There were clothes all over the floor, more dirty plates, dirty glasses, and empty beer bottles.

Munro had an idea. 'Those men must know what I look like,' he thought. Looking through the clothes on the floor, he found what he wanted – some dark green running trousers, an old Powderfinger T-shirt and some trainers that were about his size. He took off his black jeans and sweater and dressed in the new clothes. There was a baseball cap on the corner of the television. He put that on too and pulled it down over his eyes a little. Next he found a small backpack on the back of a chair. In it he put his phone, passport, money and the picture card from Longstaffe. He put the backpack on. Last, and best of all, he saw an MP3 player. He put the headphones on and the player in his trouser pocket.

The men outside were looking for someone dressed in black, someone trying to escape from them. They weren't looking for someone on holiday, someone going for an early morning run, someone who was listening to an MP3 player.

Munro looked at his watch. It was 5.30. He went to the front door and listened. He couldn't hear the men outside, but he knew they were there. He thought through his idea. 'If it doesn't work, I'm probably a dead man,' he said to himself. But just at that moment he couldn't think of anything better.

He opened the door and walked out of the flat.

There were two men standing by the door to the safe house, and two more men halfway down the stairs.

As Munro came out of the flat next door, the men looked at him for a moment and then looked away. Finding four large men outside your flat at 5.30 in the morning, most people call the police, thought Munro – so of course the men looked away. Munro closed the door behind him and then started down the stairs.

In his best New Zealand English he said 'Good day' as he passed the men on the stairs. He heard them say something; he wasn't sure what.

He made it down to the ground floor, past two more men there, and then out onto the street. Turning left, he started to run – not fast, but like someone who did this every day.

He turned the corner at the end of the street and then he started to run fast. By now the men must be in the flat and starting to think about the runner. He wanted to be a long way away and as soon as possible. As he ran, he thought. What did he need? Well, sleep for one thing. Some new clothes for another. And a car. He couldn't go back to his car. He wasn't sure that they knew about it, but it certainly wasn't a hundred per cent safe. He needed a camera too. He wanted to look at the picture card. What was so important that people were trying to kill him? And he needed a safe place to think about what to do next. As he ran, he passed the bus station. He looked at the times of buses, but the first one wasn't until 7.30. A taxi was outside the bus station. The driver was drinking coffee and reading a newspaper. Munro opened the door of the taxi.

'Where to?' asked the driver, looking at him.

Munro thought for a moment.

'Wanaka,' he said. Close to Queenstown, but far enough away to be safe for a time.

Chapter 5 *Wanaka – morning*

Wanaka is a small place right by the side of a lake of the same name. The taxi left Munro there at 6.30 in the morning. It was already light, the sun beginning to warm the waters of the lake. Munro found a seat looking over the water and sat down. His eyes closed.

Some time later something woke him. A small dog was smelling the grass around his seat. Munro watched the dog for a moment. Then he looked around. A few people were moving along the streets, one or two shops were opening – it was a small-town morning. The dog looked up at Munro and then ran off.

Munro left his seat and found a clothes shop. He bought a change of clothes – jeans, a shirt, a jacket, pants and socks, and some shoes that were the right size. He walked to the bus station, where he had a wash and changed his clothes in the men's toilet. He left the running clothes and the backpack in the toilet. Feeling better, he walked back to the town centre, where he saw the shop he was looking for. In the window were televisions, radios, computers, cameras, phones and other things. Forty-five minutes later Munro came out with a camera and a small laptop computer, both ready to use. He walked down to the lake. There was a café there, looking over the water. He sat at a table at the back of the café and, after a coffee and a full breakfast, he took out the camera. He put in the picture card and tried to find out why Longstaffe was now dead.

There were six pictures on the picture card, but Munro couldn't open them. Munro started up the laptop and moved the pictures across to the computer. He put them onto the desktop and tried again to open one. A box opened on the desktop asking him for his 'User ID'. Munro looked at it, trying to decide what to do.

'Do you mind if I sit here?' a voice asked.

Munro looked up.

The café was almost full now, and there was someone at every table. A young woman with short blonde hair, wearing a nurse's uniform under a dark blue jacket, stood in front of him. She had a cup of coffee in her hand.

'There's nowhere else to sit,' she explained. 'Can I sit here?'

'Sure,' said Munro.

The woman put her coffee on the table and sat down. Munro shut down his computer and closed it.

'Don't stop because of me,' said the woman.

'That's OK,' said Munro. 'It wasn't important.'

The woman smiled at him. She had friendly blue eyes and a nice smile.

'On holiday?' she asked.

'Something like that,' replied Munro.

The woman smiled again.

'Something like that?' she asked, her eyes still smiling. 'Well, for someone who's on holiday, you look very tired.'

'You look tired, too,' said Munro, beginning to enjoy talking to her.

'Well, as you can see, I'm a nurse,' she said, 'and I've just finished work.' She put her head a little to one side. 'What do you do?'

Munro moved a little closer to her and said quietly, 'I catch penguins. It's best to do it at night.'

The woman laughed.

Munro asked her about her job (working in a small hospital), about Wanaka (lovely place), and about where she was from (Auckland – on New Zealand's North Island and the largest town in the country). She asked him if it was difficult to catch penguins (quite), why it was best to do it at night (they were asleep) and why he did it (they were good to eat).

They laughed. Then the woman put out a hand.

'Lisa,' she said. 'Lisa Jardine.'

Munro took her hand.

'Ian Munro,' he said. 'Nice to meet you.'

Lisa Jardine finished her coffee.

'Are you staying in Wanaka?' she asked.

'I'm not really staying anywhere at the moment,' said Munro. 'I've only just arrived here.'

'Well, my flat's just round the corner,' she said, looking him in the eye. 'I'm sure I can find somewhere for you to sleep.'

* * *

Ten minutes later Lisa Jardine opened the door of her flat and walked in. Munro followed her, carrying his camera and computer. Jardine turned round and looked at him. He stopped. She moved closer to him, and put her hands up around his neck. Pulling his head down, she kissed him softly on the lips. He kissed her back. Her jacket fell to the floor, his computer and the camera onto the sofa. Her hand found its way under his shirt. His fingers pushed through her hair and he kissed her again.

'The bedroom's over there,' she said.

* * *

An hour later Lisa Jardine was sleeping quietly next to Munro. He was tired, but not yet asleep. For the moment he was safe. He was probably safer here than in a hotel, where people could find him quite easily, and certainly safer than out on the street, where people could see him. Nobody had any idea where he was – except for Lisa. In his job Munro knew it was difficult to be sure about people. But strangely he felt very sure that Lisa was OK and that she really was a nurse who didn't mind talking to a tired man in a café.

He needed to find the User ID that Longstaffe used for the information on the picture card. He could do that later. First he needed some sleep. He looked at Lisa on the bed next to him and smiled. He closed his eyes. As he slept, he dreamed of penguins: penguins running along the beach, penguins swimming underwater and catching fish, penguins at desks using computers.

Chapter 6   *Wanaka – afternoon*

Munro woke at two in the afternoon. He looked around the bedroom. Lisa was still asleep next to him. He got up and went into the living room. Outside it was a beautiful day. He went into the kitchen for a glass of water, then came back and started up his computer. As he was waiting, he looked around the room. There was a sofa, two chairs, a coffee table, a TV and a lot of photos of New Zealand on one wall. He knew where some of them were: Rotorua, Orakei Korako, the Bay of Islands, Mount Cook. Others he didn't know. Above the television was something else. He walked across the room and looked at it. 'Lisa Jardine. North Island Karate Club. Young fighter of the year,' he read. 'Interesting,' he thought.

His computer was ready. He tried again to open one of the pictures. Again a box asked him for his User ID. Munro thought for a moment. He tried 'Longstaffe'. No good. Try again. He tried 'London', 'Antarctica', 'New Zealand'. No good. They were probably too easy, he thought. Something more difficult. What did he know about Longstaffe? Not much. Nothing, actually. He thought back to the beach. What were Longstaffe's last words? Something about penguins, one-eyed penguins. He tried 'penguins'. No good. 'Penguin'. No good. 'One-eyed penguin'. No good. What did Longstaffe mean anyway? Munro stood up, walked about the room and let ideas run through his head: words, IDs, letters, numbers. Numbers, he thought. User

IDs often had letters and numbers. Did Longstaffe mean a penguin with one eye or a penguin with a 'one' for an 'i'? Munro sat down again and tried 'pengu1n'. Yes!

He opened one picture, then all the others. The pictures were all maps of the Antarctic. Munro knew some of the names: McMurdo, Vostok, Halley. These were places where scientists from the USA, Russia and Britain lived and worked. Under each name were letters and numbers. He looked at each of the maps trying to understand what the letters and numbers could be about, but they didn't mean anything to him. Why was this information so important? Longstaffe was dead because of this and now people were trying to kill him for it? Why?

Just then he heard a noise behind him. He turned round to find Lisa Jardine standing in the door, looking half asleep, wearing only a man's shirt.

'Hi,' she said. 'Have you been up long?' She came over, put her arms around him and kissed him.

'No, not long,' he replied, putting his computer to sleep.

'Something to eat?' she asked.

'Please,' he said. 'But I've got to make a phone call first.'

'The phone is over there.'

'No,' he said. 'I need to go out and make a call.' She looked at him a little strangely. 'It's better if the call doesn't come from your flat.'

'Oh! OK,' she said. Then she smiled. 'It's penguin business, is it?'

'Actually,' said Munro, smiling and thinking of the User ID on the computer, 'more so than you think.'

Munro walked down to the lake. He took out his phone. There was a danger that people might find out where he was when he turned the phone on. But 'people' really meant the police and it wasn't the police who were looking for him. Munro turned on the phone. He didn't look in the address book for Cochrane's number; he called a different number, one that he knew very well.

'This is Munro,' he said when he got through. 'I want to speak to Naylor.'

'Mr Naylor's not here at the moment, Munro,' said the voice at the other end. 'It'll take me a few minutes to find him. I've got your number. I'll get him to call you back in five minutes.'

'Fine,' said Munro.

He put the phone in his pocket and walked along the side of the lake. Two boats were out on the lake close to each other. Some young boys and girls were shouting from one boat to another, laughing, having fun.

Munro felt the phone move in his pocket. He took it out.

'Munro,' he said.

'Naylor here. What's happening?'

'I'm not sure,' replied Munro. 'I've had problems from the very start of this job.' Quickly he told Naylor about the man following him in Christchurch, about Longstaffe dying at Haast Beach and about the safe house that wasn't safe.

'Up until now they've always known where to find me,' he finished.

'How are you now?' asked Naylor.

'Free and safe,' answered Munro. No one was following him and no one knew where he was.

'You won't want to go back to Queenstown,' said Naylor.

'No,' replied Munro. 'It's a danger area for me at the moment.'

'Just a minute.'

Munro could hear Naylor talking to someone else. Then he came back to the phone.

'How about Dunedin?' asked Naylor.

'It'll take four or five hours to get there, but that's not a problem.'

'Go to the Moray Hotel in the centre of town,' said Naylor. 'Get there as soon as you can. Ask for Mr Broadhurst.'

'Understood.'

Munro turned off the phone and put it back in his pocket.

* * *

Back at Lisa Jardine's flat, food was on the kitchen table – breakfast, but at three in the afternoon. Jardine was standing, drinking coffee, as Munro came into the kitchen. She put her cup down on the table. Her eyes took in Munro's dark brown, almost black hair.

'Breakfast?' she asked, smiling into his light grey eyes.

Munro smiled back.

'Sounds good,' he replied.

Jardine put her hand on his arm and looked up at him.

'Or …?' It was only half a question.

Munro looked down at her blue eyes, put his hand on the back of her neck and pulled her to him.

'Yes,' he said. 'Maybe a bit later.' He put his other arm around her and then kissed her softly.

* * *

Some time later Munro was lying next to Lisa Jardine on her bed.

'How's your karate?' he asked.

'Oh! You saw that – above the television.' Jardine laughed. 'Actually my karate's not bad. I was second best in the South Island last year. Why? Do you want a fight?'

It was Munro's turn to laugh.

'No, thanks,' he said. 'You might win.'

Lisa turned her head and gave him a long look.

'I don't think so,' she said. 'I get the feeling you know how to look after yourself.'

Munro turned onto on his stomach, his head up, looking down at her.

'I really have to go soon,' he said. 'And I need a car. Is there somewhere in Wanaka I can get one?'

'I've got one,' she replied. 'And I'm not working this evening. I could drive you.'

'That's kind of you,' he said, looking at her, 'but probably not a good idea.'

'OK,' said Jardine. 'Then there's Stewart's Autos. Look out of the window. You'll see it down the street on the right. Near the town centre.'

Munro got up and went over to the window. Looking out and to the right Munro could just see Stewart's Autos. He could also see a lot of tourists out on the streets of Wanaka. Munro watched them for a few moments. But then something caught his eye: a tall man, wearing a dark suit and dark glasses. Not a tourist. He was standing outside a shop and looking first one way and then the other. A second man came up to him, also in a suit, but without the sunglasses. The first man took something like a piece of paper out of his pocket and they both looked at it. Munro was too far away to see what it was. But then one of the men stopped a woman who was walking past. He showed her the paper and asked her a question. 'That's not a piece of paper, that's a photo,' thought Munro. 'And those men are looking for me.'

Lisa Jardine was watching him from the bed.

'What is it?' she asked.

Munro thought fast. The men were looking for one man, not a man and a woman together. Maybe using Jardine's car was a good idea after all.

'Actually,' he said, 'I've changed my mind. Let's use your car. And let's go now.'

Chapter 7   *From Wanaka to Dunedin*

Quickly Munro and Jardine dressed. He had the clothes he bought that morning. She put on jeans, a light-green T-shirt and trainers. He took his computer and the camera and she took a small shoulder bag. Luckily her car was right in front of the building. No one saw them. They got in the car and, with Jardine at the wheel, they drove all the way along Brownston Street. Jardine felt, rather than knew, that it was best to stay away from the busy tourist area by the side of the lake. She looked quickly at Munro, but didn't say anything. She knew something was wrong, but she also knew it was not the right time to ask questions.

Munro was thinking, asking himself how they knew where he was. It had to be the phone calls. That was the only way. They could be looking for him in a number of different towns, but Munro didn't think so. They knew he was in Wanaka, but they didn't know where.

'But if that's how they know,' thought Munro, 'then that's very interesting. It means they're probably working with the police in some way. Or maybe a police officer is working with them.'

Jardine stopped at the end of the street, waiting for cars to pass. Munro looked left and saw the bus station. A tourist bus was waiting by the side of the road. The side of the bus was open and the driver was putting tourists' bags into it.

Munro had an idea. 'Mobile phones can make problems for them as well as me,' he thought, and smiled to himself.

'Turn left,' he said to Jardine. 'And stop behind the bus.'

Jardine pulled over to the side of the road. Munro got out of the car. He took his phone out of his pocket and turned it on.

The driver was busy with the tourists' bags when Munro walked up. Munro still had his phone in his hand.

'Sorry,' said Munro, looking into the side of the bus where all the bags were. 'I forgot to lock my bag.'

'No problem,' said the driver. He turned to get another bag.

Munro put his hand down between two bags and left the phone there.

'Thanks,' said Munro to the driver. He stood up again and then quickly walked to the front of the bus so the driver thought he was getting on. But he didn't. He went round the front and back to Jardine's car.

'What was all that about?' asked Lisa Jardine when he got back in the car.

'I was just making work for some people,' replied Munro and smiled at her.

'Now that the phone is on the bus they'll think I'm on the bus too,' he thought. Jardine drove past the bus and Munro looked back. It said 'Christchurch' on the front of the bus.

'Good,' thought Munro. 'The wrong way.'

'Where to?' asked Jardine.

'Dunedin,' said Munro. 'Is that OK?'

'Fine,' replied Jardine. 'It's a nice drive.'

'I'll tell you a bit about penguins on the way,' said Munro.

* * *

They took the road out towards Dunedin. Munro liked the way Jardine drove – safe but not slow. On the way he told her a little about his job. What he said was almost true. He told her he was a businessman. He had some important information which he needed to get back to Britain, but there were other people who wanted the information. And they wanted it badly.

'Can't you just email it home?' asked Jardine.

'Email really isn't safe,' answered Munro. 'An email doesn't always go where you want it to go.'

'True,' said Jardine. 'So why are we going to Dunedin?'

'My boss is sending me there to meet someone. Someone who can help.'

They sat for a moment without talking.

Then Lisa Jardine spoke: 'Well, it's a better story than catching penguins,' she said, smiling. 'But you still haven't told me everything.'

Munro smiled too.

'You know enough,' he said.

* * *

It was ten o'clock at night when they drove into Dunedin. It was raining and the streets were almost empty. It was dark now, but Munro remembered it as a grey city in the daytime. The name Dunedin means Edinburgh in the Celtic language and Munro thought that in many ways the city was very like his home town of Edinburgh. Some of the buildings looked the same; some of the street names were the same; and some of the weather was just the same.

'Where are we going?' asked Jardine.

'The Moray Hotel,' replied Munro. 'Do you know it?'

'I know where it is,' said Jardine. 'Everyone does. It's *the* hotel in Dunedin.'

'OK,' said Munro. 'That's where I'm going. But let's just drive past it first. I want to see if there's anyone there waiting for me.'

They drove along Princes Street and then left into Moray Place. They drove past the front doors of the Moray Hotel. Munro sat well down in his seat looking out on both sides of the street. There were few people out in the rain. Most of them were hurrying home out of the wet. Nobody was watching or waiting.

'Let's do that again,' said Munro.

They drove past again, this time coming from the other way. Again Munro looked out on both sides. Nothing – no danger that he could see.

'OK,' he said. 'This time stop somewhere as close to the hotel as you can. I'll get out. You stay in the car.'

'You're joking,' replied Jardine. 'I'm not staying in the car at this time of night. I'm coming into the hotel with you. I'll stay downstairs, if you like, and you can go and see this person. But I'm not staying in the car.'

Munro looked at her. He knew he couldn't make her stay in the car and it was raining more heavily now.

'Fine,' he said.

Jardine stopped the car near the front of the hotel. They got out quickly and ran in through the front door.

Just inside on the left was the front desk. At the back of the room there was the sound of voices from the bar area, and on the right were chairs, tables, newspapers and an open fire. Two groups of people were sitting at tables talking.

'That looks good to me,' said Jardine, seeing the open fire. 'I'll wait here and read the paper. You go and talk penguin business.'

'OK,' said Munro. He didn't smile. He was looking around the room to see if anyone was watching them. Everything looked fine. He turned to the man behind the front desk.

'I'm looking for Mr Broadhurst,' he said.

'Room 326, sir. Third floor. Can I call him for you?'

'That's OK,' replied Munro. 'He knows I'm coming.'

Munro took the stairs to the third floor and knocked on the door of room 326.

The door opened and there, standing in front of him, was the one person Munro didn't think was in New Zealand – Naylor.

Chapter 8 *Dunedin*

'What the … What are you doing here?' asked Munro, closing the door behind him.

'Take a seat, Munro,' said Naylor, going to a chair by the window and sitting down. There was a glass of beer on the table next to him. 'Actually, I've been in New Zealand for the last three weeks.'

Munro's mouth fell open. 'But …'

'I know,' said Naylor. 'People say I never leave the country. I like people to think that, but it's not true. When a job is very important and I need to be there, I go.'

Munro sat down. 'And this job …' he began.

'… is very important,' finished Naylor. 'By the way, I've asked for some sandwiches and coffee.'

Munro was thinking fast. He had a lot of questions, but he waited. Naylor didn't tell people what they wanted to know. He told them what they needed to know.

'We're working together with the SCI on this. The SCI is part of the New Zealand police. They look at difficult problems outside usual police work. And the SCI and us, we're both looking at different areas of the same problem.'

Munro looked questioningly at Naylor. He didn't understand.

'Their problem is a group of about nine men, some New Zealanders and some from a number of different countries in central Asia,' Naylor went on. 'The SCI believe, actually they know, that these men are all spies. They've known this for two or three years. These spies work for one country, but they're also getting information and selling it to other countries. The SCI want to catch the spies and send them all to prison.'

'And our problem?' asked Munro.

'Our problem,' said Naylor, 'is Cochrane.'

'Ah!' said Munro. 'I thought so.'

'Yes,' said Naylor. 'That's why someone followed you from the airport. That's why there were people waiting for you on Haast Beach. That's why the safe house wasn't safe. Cochrane was telling them where you were. Cochrane is working with these people. Actually, it looks as if he's their boss.' Naylor took a drink of beer.

'How long have you known about Cochrane?' asked Munro.

'That he was working for someone else as well as us? I wasn't sure until you called me earlier,' replied Naylor. 'But I've thought it for a long time. The SCI found out Cochrane was one of us and started asking me questions. I told them what I knew, and what I thought, and they asked us to work with them so that together we could catch him. They had enough information on all the other people in the group to send them to prison, but very little on Cochrane.'

'He must be cleverer than I thought,' said Munro.

'Yes,' agreed Naylor. 'Anyway, we just had to wait for the right time and the right job. And this information from the Antarctic was what I needed.'

Munro stayed quiet. He was thinking about the last forty-eight hours.

'You've done an excellent job,' said Naylor. 'We can now be sure that Cochrane is working against us. And the men who followed you in Christchurch, the ones who were at Haast Beach, and the ones in Queenstown – they're all working for him.'

'They were in Wanaka too,' said Munro.

'Tell me,' said Naylor.

Quickly Munro told Naylor about his time in Wanaka and the men with the photograph on the street just before he left.

Naylor listened and then spoke: 'One of the New Zealanders in the group is a police officer. He probably found out where you were when you called me.'

'That's what I decided too,' replied Munro and told Naylor how he put his phone on the bus for Christchurch.

Naylor smiled and took another drink of beer.

'Anyway,' asked Munro. 'What next?'

'Well, the SCI are still watching these men. As I said, they already have enough information to send them all to prison. They can bring them in at any time. But if they do, Cochrane could get away – so they are giving us time to catch him. And I want to catch him. For Longstaffe as much as anything else. Longstaffe was a good man.'

'Where is Cochrane?' asked Munro.

'No one has seen him since he met you at the airport.'

'He must still be in New Zealand if he wants to get Longstaffe's information,' said Munro.

'You still have the picture card, do you?' asked Naylor.

'Yes,' answered Munro.

'Good,' said Naylor. 'You could need it. Your job now is to find Cochrane and catch him.'

Just then they heard someone at the door.

'Sandwiches and coffee for room 326,' said a voice.

Munro stood up, walked over to the door and opened it. A hand pushed him back into the room and Munro almost fell over. Cochrane came quickly into the room, shutting the door behind him. There was a gun in his hand and a smile on his face.

'Good evening, Munro,' he said. And then, seeing Naylor, his mouth fell open. Quickly he shut it. For a moment there was a strange angry look in his eyes, but then he smiled. 'And it's the old man himself, Mr Naylor – I certainly didn't think you'd be here. This rather changes things.'

He waved his gun at Munro.

'Sit down, Munro. I don't want any funny business.'

Chapter 9 *The end of the road*

'How did you find me, Cochrane?' asked Munro. He stayed standing. He wanted to be on his feet if he could.

'You're not as clever as you think you are, Munro,' said Cochrane. 'Putting your phone on the bus was a good idea, but not quite good enough. Now, sit down I said.'

Munro sat down on the very front of the chair, his legs well back under him. All he needed was a second or two and he could push off hard and get to Cochrane. But at the moment Cochrane was watching him carefully.

Cochrane started talking again. 'He really wants us to know how clever he is,' thought Munro.

'Of course, my men are very good,' explained Cochrane. 'We lost you after Queenstown, but then you made that phone call. Stupid mistake, really, Munro. And, as soon as you did that, we knew you were in Wanaka.'

Munro looked at Naylor. He was sitting back in his chair, the glass of beer in his hand and a half-smile on his face.

'Two of the men went after the bus to Christchurch, but I knew you were cleverer than that. We wanted to know what you were doing in Wanaka, who you were seeing. And we found out.'

Munro said nothing. He watched the gun in Cochrane's hand. It didn't move.

'We found Ms Jardine's flat, her car number and then her car – right outside this hotel. It's not too difficult if you have the right people working for you,' laughed Cochrane. 'But now, since my men are having problems getting what I want, I've come to finish the job myself.'

Just then there was a noise at the door and it opened. Into the room came Lisa Jardine. Behind her was a tall, dark man with black hair and a gun in his hand.

'Ah!' said Cochrane, looking at the door and then very quickly back at Munro. 'Here is the lovely Ms Jardine, and with her Mr Safarian. Mr Safarian is a cousin of Mr Krikorian, who you met in Christchurch.'

Munro's face didn't move. He watched Cochrane.

'Where was she?' Cochrane asked Safarian.

'In the bar,' replied Safarian.

'I understand Mr Safarian wants to spend a little time with you later, Munro.' Cochrane laughed again. 'He's very unhappy about what you did to his cousin.'

Munro looked at where everyone was in the room. He could get to Cochrane, but he needed time. Not much, just a second or two. Lisa Jardine was very close to Safarian. Naylor was still in his chair on Munro's right.

'Right,' said Cochrane. 'Down to business.'

Munro looked at Lisa Jardine and caught her eye.

'Are you OK, Lisa?' he asked.

'Fine,' she said. Her voice was strong, and there was still some colour in her face. 'Good,' thought Munro. But he needed to let her know what he wanted her to do.

'Longstaffe's information,' said Cochrane. 'Where is it?'

Nobody spoke.

'Mr Safarian,' said Cochrane.

Safarian put his gun against the side of Lisa Jardine's head.

'Give him what he wants.' It was Naylor. 'We don't want any shooting in the hotel.'

'OK,' said Munro. He looked at Safarian. 'Put that gun down,' he said, 'and I'll give it to you.'

Safarian looked at Cochrane.

'OK,' said Cochrane.

Safarian moved the gun down a little.

'It's in my pocket,' said Munro. He didn't want Cochrane shooting him because he put a hand in his pocket.

Cochrane smiled.

'That's OK,' he said. 'I know you never carry a gun.'

Munro put his hand in his pocket. At the same time he spoke to Lisa Jardine.

'Lisa, you know what you're second best at.'

She didn't have to think for long. She knew what he was talking about.

'Yes,' she replied.

'Shut up!' It was Cochrane.

Munro saw the light in Lisa Jardine's eyes. He knew she understood. Her body moved just a little as she got ready.

Munro's hand came out of his pocket with the picture card in it. He knew he had to get this just right – he needed time to get to Cochrane. His hand moved and the picture card went up in the air. Cochrane's eyes followed it.

Munro came off the chair like an Olympic runner at the start of the hundred metres. One hand hit Cochrane's gun away to the left. The gun flew out of his hand and broke the glass of a picture on the wall. Munro's other hand shot into Cochrane's stomach. There was a small noise as the air left his body and he fell to the floor.

Across the room Lisa Jardine moved at the same time as Munro. She turned quickly, pushing Safarian's gun to the side with one hand, her other hand hitting him hard on the nose. Safarian cried out and moved back. This gave Jardine the room she needed. Her foot came up hard between his legs. Safarian cried out again, his head came down and Jardine hit him hard again in the face with her knee. He fell to the floor and didn't move.

Cochrane was moving on the floor, making noises, trying to get air back into his body. Munro got down on one knee, took off Cochrane's belt and tied his hands behind his back.

He looked across the room and saw Lisa Jardine doing the same to Safarian. Naylor was making a call.

'Inspector Howarth, SCI, please,' he said. He didn't have to wait long to get through. Munro and Jardine heard

Naylor's side of the conversation.

'Howarth, this is Naylor. We're all finished here. The men you're watching – you can bring them in now. We've got Cochrane here and another man – Safarian ... OK ... Yes, that's right ... Not at all.' Naylor put the phone down.

Munro looked on the floor and found the picture card. He took it and gave it to Naylor.

'You probably want this, sir.'

'Yes.' Naylor looked at the card and turned it over in his hand. 'Not that it's any use to anyone,' he said.

'What do you mean?' asked Munro.

'Did you have a look at it?' asked Naylor.

'Yes,' answered Munro, 'but I didn't understand it.'

'There was nothing to understand,' replied Naylor. 'There wasn't much information on it at all – well, nothing you couldn't find on the internet.'

'But ...' began Munro.

'Cochrane believed it was important. He thought it was so important that he used nine other men to try and get it for his employers. But it was just cheese, really – a piece of cheese to catch a mouse – or rather a rat,' he said looking down at Cochrane.

Munro smiled to himself. It was a great idea of Naylor's: catching Cochrane with unimportant information. Something for nothing. It was dangerous for him, Munro, but that was why he did this job. For those moments when life felt real: waiting for a cloud to move across the moon, escaping through the roof of a strange house, meeting smiling blue eyes in an early-morning café, looking into the face of danger and not turning away. Today he was lucky. Lucky and alive. The next job could be different.

'And Longstaffe?' asked Munro.

'Yes, I'm angry about that,' replied Naylor. 'Angry that his life meant so little to some people.' He gave Cochrane a dark look as he spoke. 'And I'm truly sorry,' continued Naylor. 'Like I said, he was a good man. But *you* know – everyone who works for me knows – that there are dangers in this job. Very real dangers.'

Naylor stood up and looked at Lisa Jardine and then at Munro.

'You can go, Munro,' he said. 'The SCI will be here soon to take these two away. I'll wait for them. You need to take Ms Jardine home, I think. And, anyway, you're on holiday.'

* * *

Outside, they walked to Lisa Jardine's car and got in. Munro looked across at her.

'Thank you,' he said, 'for what you did back there.'

'That's OK,' she said. Her hands were on the wheel, but she didn't start the car. 'Naylor's a hard man, isn't he?' she said. 'And your job can actually be very dangerous.'

At first Munro just looked ahead and said nothing. Then he said, 'Yes, Naylor is hard. But he's also very good at what he does. And it's important work that we do – important for our country and the people who live in it.'

'Yes,' said Lisa, 'I can see that.' She started the car.

'You're really on holiday now, are you?' she asked.

'Yes.'

'Where were you thinking of going?' she asked.

'I've heard about somewhere called Wanaka. Do you think it's a good place to go?'

'There's only one way to find out,' said Lisa Jardine, with a smile.